OUR FORGOTTEN NORTH

A GLIMPSE OF THE SUBARCTIC IN CANADA'S NORTH

by

LESLIE LEONG

Dedicated to my son Tynan, with the hope
that wild spaces like these will survive for
his generation to be a part of in the future.

Leslie
Leong ENT.
LTD.

A muskox stretches after waking from a midday sleep in the Thelon Wildlife Sanctuary. The mainland muskoxen population was nearly hunted to extinction by 1900, but today many thousand animals thrive under protection.

Published in Canada by Leslie Leong Ent. Ltd.
Box 1372, Fort Smith, Northwest Territories   XOE OPO

Canadian Cataloguing in Publication Data

Leong, Leslie, 1962 -

      Our Forgotten North: a glimpse of the subarctic in Canada's north.

ISBN 0-9681715-0-8

      1. Canada, Northern — Pictorial works. 2. Natural History — Canada, Northern — Pictorial works. 3. Canada, Northern — Description and travel. I. Title

FC3956.L46 1997   917.19'0022'2   C96-901082-6
F1090.5.L 46 1997

Printed and bound in Canada.

Cover Photo: *Nahanni Butte, viewed across the Liard River from Blackstone Territorial Park.*

Title Page Photos: *The rock cranberry is one of the most relished edible northern plants. Their berries ripen after the first frosts and are reputedly most delectable in the spring, after having past the long winter under the snow.*

ACKNOWLEDGMENTS

I wish to express my deep appreciation to all those who have given their support and encouragement during the two years it took to plan and produce Our Forgotten North.

For their essential support in the tourism sector: The Government of the Northwest Territories' Department of Renewable Resources, Wildlife and Economic Development, especially John Sheehan of the South Slave Region; Robert Nowosad, DehCho Region; Lloyd Binder and Judith Venus, Inuvik Region; Larry Adamson and Barry Stoneman, North Slave Region; Robin Reilly and James Smyth, Headquarters. Also to Ann Ward and the Big River Tourism Association, and Sam Ransom.

All those that supported the photographic exhibit that gave birth to this project: NWT Arts Council, Great Northern Arts Festival, Festival of the Midnight Sun, Wally Wolfe, Prince of Wales Northern Heritage Centre, Northern Life Museum, Marilyn Barnes, Hay River Public Library, Jack Rowe, Heather Don-Gullickson, Fort Simpson Visitor Centre, and everyone who wrote encouraging notes in the comment book. Thanks also to the late Hank Colborne for his encouraging support.

Adventure companions who endured while I took the time to get just the right shots: Lillian Leong, Terry Best, Linda Calder, Charlie Bourque, Heather Swystun, Janet & George Mercer, Libby Gunn, Blair & Kelley Best, Colin Bonnycastle, and many others.

For their advice, technical knowledge, and guidance: Kim Kuzak, Mark Bradley, Alex Hall, JC Catholique, John Cournoyea, Peggy Jay, Kevin & Rita Antoniak, Jane Chisholm, Don Lemmen, Jenny Wilson, Larry Gray, Tom Andrews, Ib Kristensen of North of 60 Books; Judith Drinnan of The YK Book Cellar; and Dick Hill of Boreal Books.

The organizations and many individuals who have supported my photographic endeavors over the years: Big River Air Ltd., Canoe Arctic Inc., Don Aubrey, Jean Boxer, Bill Wade and many more.

Special thanks to Pat & Rosemarie Keough whose faith in my photography gave me the confidence to pursue this project and whose guidance has been invaluable throughout.

My only regret is not having enough space to acknowledge everyone on this project.

Autumn display of colour in the subarctic foliage of poplar, willow, fire-weed and high-bush cranberry.

The serene beauty of sunlight and shadows draws adventurers out into the frozen environment of the subarctic winter. Despite the long cold winter, water remains open at Cassette Rapids on the Slave River and sends mist into the air. The mist then settles as frost on the nearby trees.

INTRODUCTION

The sensation begins the moment the Cessna 185 detaches itself from the clinging surface of the water and begins to climb into the limitless sky. My umbilical cord to the comfortable world of modern civilization has been severed. The whine of the engine gradually fades as the plane becomes a small dot in the distance, then disappears completely. The sensation is building: anxiety, finality and a sense of emptiness sink deeper and deeper into my body, penetrating my soul, my very existence.

My mother and I are left standing beside our small heap of gear, 450 kilometres from the closest human settlement, with no way to contact the outside world. In 22 days the float plane will meet us at a pre-determined location 320 kilometres down river to take us home from this remote and awe-inspiring wilderness.

My anxiety fades as silence begins to fill my deep emptiness. Warm sun, chilled by a north wind sweeping off the tundra, touches my face. The sweet fragrant smell of Labrador tea blossoms warming in the late morning sun greets my nose. Around me is an incredible expanse of sky and a land sparsely dotted with scrubby clumps of spruce. It all pours into me, through every one of my senses. It is like a rebirth, an awakening to the natural world, a profoundly spiritual and healing experience. I feel complete, content, present in the here and now. I am at one with the natural world, part of the whole.

I think about that. Humans *are* part of the natural world but our industrialized society severs the connection and makes us uncertain of our place. I am relieved to leave behind the detached existence of urban society, that place where we live in our heads but not in our hearts. I am happy to be fulfilled again.

Each time I journey into the wilds of this great land, I feel a sense of reconnection to the earth. "Our Forgotten North" is my way of sharing this experience with you, with all humanity, for the sake of humanity. It is a journey of adventure, discovery and spiritual connection to the wild and stunningly beautiful subarctic. Meet the wildlife, the people and the awesome scenery through photographs, personal experiences and natural history.

The Forgotten North is a zone of ecological transition in which thick boreal forests at the northern edge of the treeline gradually dissolve into small clumps of gnarled spruce on the open tundra. The land is filled with unforgettable treasures, many unique in Canada and the world, ranging from the intricate detail of minute yet vibrant pink blossoms of moss campion to the magnificent grandeur of Virginia Falls and dazzling autumn vistas in the Richardson Mountains. The land abounds with wildlife, from prehistoric-looking muskox to elusive wolf, masses of caribou to playfully curious river otter, and delicate yet enduring arctic tern to predatory great horned owl.

Subarctic seasons are distinct and dramatic: long, warm summer days, when dusk turns to dawn and temperatures rise above 30°C; equally long but cold winter nights, when temperatures can fall below -40°C and the skies are filled with the majestic northern lights, illuminating the darkness with a flurry of spectacular activity. Spring and autumn are brief and exciting, filled with rapid change.

Aboriginal peoples make up the majority of the sparse population. Over centuries, they have developed a way of life that is intimately intertwined with the land and all it supports, a way of life that considers humans a part of nature that must live within and respect natural laws. Aboriginal cultures date back more than 8,000 years, long before the first Europeans arrived in the 1700s.

The Forgotten North extends from the northern extremes of Canada's western provinces, beginning in the dazzling sand dunes on the south shore of Lake Athabasca and proceeding to where the waters of the lake feed the mighty Slave River, then gradually curving northwest along the treeline, through the great Salt Plains in Wood Buffalo National Park and past the Slave River rapids, gateway to the north.

Beginning deep in the boreal forest, this subarctic land passes through a series of plummeting waterfalls and magnificent river canyons, then spans the treeline through the Taiga Shield, with its great rock outcrops, wind-blown conifers, rushing rivers and crystal clear lakes, including the immense Great Slave Lake and its cliff-bordered East Arm. The north-east of the Forgotten North is the "place where god began," the last pocket of trees isolated by open tundra that makes up the Thelon Wildlife Sanctuary. Following the Mackenzie drainage north by northwest takes us into the land of majestic mountains and mythical rivers and finally to the disorienting maze of the Mackenzie Delta and the scenic Dempster Highway, the most northerly road link to the south.

The incredibly diverse subarctic is often forgotten when people read and talk about the Canadian north. It is not home to polar bears, icebergs or Inuit seal hunters. The Forgotten North is something different, a place most of us know little about. It is isolated and inaccessible, yet more accessible than the high arctic and therefore threatened by development. Although development is so far dwarfed by the vastness of this remote land, there is concern among the people of the Forgotten North. Many cherish the pristine nature of this wild and virtually untouched land, and fear politicians enamoured by "Roads to Resources" will bring a wave of industrial and mining development.

Today, Canadians have the chance to preserve huge tracts of land where plants and wildlife live undisturbed, where nature and ecology play out timeless processes free from human intervention. The Forgotten North is one of the last places on earth with vast expanses of uninhabited land that can still be put aside for enjoyment by all earth's creatures.

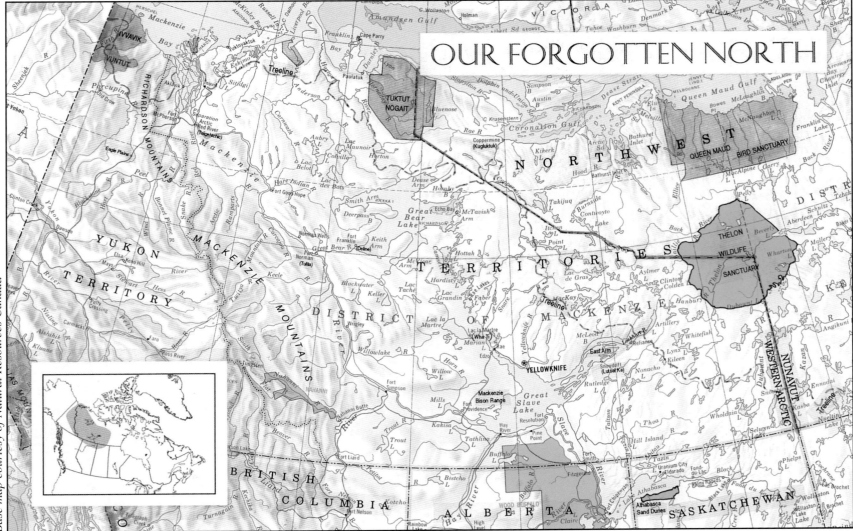

OUR FORGOTTEN NORTH

Base map courtesy of Natural Resources Canada

White pelicans spend long summer days bobbing for fish in the calmer rapids of the Slave River. This most northerly colony of white pelicans is the only one in the world that nests on river islands protected by raging whitewater - too dangerous for even the most experienced whitewater kayak enthusiasts or river rafters.

The subarctic is an ecological transition zone filled with an abundance of wildlife, including rare species like the whooping crane, white pelican and wood bison. Populations of these threatened species have recently stabilized and even begun to recover, assisted by special protected areas and the remoteness and undisturbed state of the Forgotten North.

In 1941 there were only 21 whooping cranes left in the world but with the help of dedicated biologists and the preservation of their secluded summer nesting grounds in and around Wood Buffalo National Park, the whooping crane is making a comeback. Today there are 261 of these magnificent birds, with a wild population of 133 nesting in these northerly wetlands and wintering in the Aransas Refuge in Texas. The whooping crane is North America's tallest bird, with a wing span of two metres or more, a standing height of 1.5 metres and a weight of 7.5 kilograms.

Before European settlement, white pelicans nested throughout much of western North America. Conservation efforts were initiated by a sudden, massive decline thought to be caused by widespread use of toxic chemicals. Populations have since rebounded and the white pelican was removed from the endangered species list in 1987. The number of nests on the Slave River near Fort Smith has grown from 25 to over 300 in just twenty years.

Wood bison historically ranged north to Lac la Martre and south to the Rocky Mountain foothills in Colorado. By 1891 fewer than 300 animals remained, mainly in the present day Wood Buffalo National Park. Interbreeding with introduced plains bison increased over all numbers but also brought cattle diseases to the herds. Later a few disease free animals with original wood bison features were relocated further north to the Mackenzie Bison Range, where 1300 bison now live. Another 2700 bison roam the Wood Buffalo area, where human intervention remains a threat. Ranchers are concerned that bison may return the diseases to their now disease-free cattle, although research indicates this is unlikely.

Upper: *The threat display of a common loon defending its territory.*
Lower: *Bunchberry blossoms become brilliant red clusters of berries in late summer and fall. They are also known as dwarf dogwood.*

Wild herds of bison roam free in the Mackenzie Bison Range, the South Nahanni, the Slave River Lowlands, and Wood Buffalo National Park.

Upper: *This pictograph near Fort Smith was strategically left by Crees pursued by Dogribs, who mysteriously abandoned the chase after seeing it.*
Lower: *Moonrise at the float plane base marks the end of a wilderness journey.*

Upper: *Dust lingers after a roll in a wallow. The farther a bison can roll over on his hump, the greater the display of strength to other bulls during the rut.*
Lower: *Paddling with a canine passenger in the late summer midnight sun.*

A wild rose finds nourishment in the decaying foliage and deadfall of seasons past.

The brown, silt-laden Slave River is transformed into an upheaval of whitewater as it tumbles from Fort Fitzgerald to Fort Smith. Four sets of rapids are formed over a 25 kilometre stretch as the Canadian Shield pinches the immense flow of the river, revealing extremes of both beauty and power.

The rapids are the only major obstacle to navigation along the water route between southern Canada and the Arctic Ocean. Most traders chose a long portage around this "gateway to the north" rather than risk losing precious cargo, while natives, early explorers and fur traders used a well-established series of shorter portages down the east side of the river. Modern travelers can follow the historic eastern route through calmer water between islands, down small twisted side channels, and over well-worn portage trails.

Blue-eyed grass, like many boreal flowers, are jewels of vibrant colour, rising up from the thick green mat of the forest floor.

At the edge of the rapids, serenity is attained in a pool of water stranded by the declining level of the Slave River in autumn.

The wild whitewater of the Slave River rapids was a major obstacle to the trappers, traders and natives, who travelled north with supplies and south with furs. The earliest portage routes were well established by the late 1700's and can still be travelled today.

Upper: *Mudstone concretions are formed by the cementation of sediment by silica. These disc-shaped treasures are revealed as the Slave River recedes in autumn.*
Lower: *Rafting enthusiasts pick their way along less hazardous routes of the rapids.*

A hardy, yet delicate fern takes hold in a crack of a granite outcrop, where fine grains of soil, decaying plant matter and moisture are harboured.

Gull chicks spend spring in nests on islands along the Slave River rapids, protected from predators unable to access these island sanctuaries.

A young great horned owl is surprised by the sight of a fellow visitor to the falls. Although this dominant avian predator possesses a keen sense of hearing, the roar of the falls made it possible for me to approach without detection.

Wind bound camp at the far reaches of the treeline. More valuable than gold, the Thelon Wildlife Sanctuary can be found at the end of this rainbow.

Upper: *Nesting swallows find natural protection from weather and predators in the karst bluffs of the Salt River near Fort Smith.*
Lower: *The midnight sun casts shadows of clustered spruce on the tent door.*

The pasque-flower, or wild crocus, pushes through the chaotic mass of decomposing foliage from autumn past. It is the first flower to emerge after the snow has melted.

Upper: *Bush planes are an important link to the remote wilderness of the north.*
Lower: *Yellow water lily after the rain. An important food source for muskrat and beaver, it can be found in many ponds, shallow lakes and sluggish streams.*

Drying fish at a Dene camp. Preparation of the fish includes meticulous cleaning and cutting to facilitate fast, even drying. Sometimes it is smoked over a smudge fire using wood specially selected for smoldering.

The Dene people have a long history of living on the land. Today they continue to harvest caribou, moose, beaver, fish and birds for food and clothing, as well as berries, mint, rat root, chamomile and birch bark for food, medicinal remedies and other useful items.

Hides are tanned using a traditional process that produces a more durable, stronger, lighter and warmer material than commercially tanned hides. Both sides of the hide are scraped to remove flesh and hair, and to thin the hide. The hide is soaked in an oily substance, such as brains, then smoked and worked to break down the fibers and soften the material. The process is physically laborious, with each of the steps taking days to complete.

Food and products made from natural sources have an inherent spiritual value and are considered to be of higher quality and durability.

Out on the land, elders use a bed of dwarf birch leaves to lay a midday meal of dry fish, bannock and tea.

Upper: *Hung fish from the fall run are used in winter to feed sled dogs.*
Lower: *Birch bark, porcupine quills and tanned hides and fur are used to make mittens, moccasins, berry baskets and other items.*

Maintaining ancient tradition, Dene drummers tighten the hides on their drums over the camp fire and summon the power of the ancestral spirit.

Upper: *Dene drums are made with birch wood, caribou hide, and sinew.*
Lower: *Crafted from home-tanned moose hide, these moccasins are far more durable than products made from commercially tanned hides.*

Drumming initiates a spiritual connection between the Dene and the Creator during a celebration, healing circle or sweat lodge, or the commemoration of a death and subsequent journey to the next world. Together with song, drumming is essentially a form of prayer. Special events and meetings are opened by prayer, and early morning drumming and singing put the Creator ahead of everything else.

The drum is a spiritual tool and must be respected and handled accordingly. Its keeper must follow spiritual laws and live an undefiled life. During a drum dance, spirituality is sensed by all. The beat of the drum and the chant of the song inspire people to get up and join the dancing circle.

The songs of the drum dance are also for entertainment and amusement during journeys out on the land.

My approach distracts a red fox from digging up her food cache. I surprised the animal with her face buried in the snow sniffing out the goods. Her thick coat is evidence of a winter abundant in good food sources.

For a few short weeks, trembling aspen shimmer brilliant oranges and yellows in the autumn winds, like many tambourines.

Bears, wolves, moose and bison are among the large mammals attracted to the salt deposits to lick this mineral so vital to their diet.

Upper: *Wildlife tracks, like these of the sandhill crane, add to the patterns of cracks and eroded boulders littering the mud flats of Grosbeak Lake.*
Lower: *Texture and scale in the mud near the end of a long dry summer.*

The ever-changing environment of Grosbeak Lake near Fort Smith displays precipitated salt after a long dry spell. Salt accelerates the erosion of the erratics, boulders left behind by glaciers. Together with years of freeze-thaw action, this process breaks down the weaker layers and pockets to create wonderfully weird shapes. Granular in texture, the granite boulders display contorted surfaces, sweeping grooves, gaping hollows, gouges and deep cavities.

oft mud oozes up to my knees as I gaze out over the Salt Plains, trying to get a true sense of the place. Bright red samphire and golden yellow Nuttall's meadow grass line the alternating mud flats. Patches of dwarf birch, yellow and orange from the first frost, add relief to the foreground, while clusters of spruce punctuate the sky-line. Fluffy white clouds reflect off the placid, shallow waters, as sandpiper calls pierce the silence.

In another stretch of the plains, Grosbeak Lake comprises the muddy remnants of a once-large lake, and adds its unique features to the salty landscape. Cracks in the drying mud and lines of salt precipitate create a jigsaw puzzle pattern, criss-crossed by the tracks of birds, animals and humans. The mud flats are dotted with glacial erratics eroded into bizarre and fantastic shapes by salt and freezing temperatures. Hundreds of gulls nest at the centre of the lake, protected by water and deep mud.

A natural spring bubbles to the earth's surface. This water is so heavily saturated, salt precipitates even under the water.

In depressions and along cracks and streams, the salt saturation increases in the water with evaporation, leaving salt precipitate in its wake.

Salt water has flowed onto the Salt Plains for thousands of years, creating an unusual vegetation community. Salt tolerant and salt resistant plants have evolved over time, lining the edges of mud flats and establishing vegetation islands of salt-stressed spruce. The bare mud flats themselves are too saline to support vegetation.

The salt was originally left behind when vast ancient seas dried up 270 million years ago. Thousands of feet of sedimentary rock cover the salt beds in other parts of the prairies but here they are much closer to the surface. Groundwater flows through the subterranean salt beds and is then forced upward by the bedrock of the Interior Plains butting against the granite of the Canadian Shield. Once at the surface, the water evaporates in the summer heat. Some salt is left in crystalline mounds at the outflow of springs, while the rest is distributed across the plains and into nearby waterways.

The Slavey, Beaver, Chipewyan, and Cree people have harvested crystalline salt from the plains for hundreds of years. Salt was gathered, pounded and used to preserve fish, waterfowl and wild game. Following the arrival of the Hudson's Bay Company and the Northwest Company, salt was distributed throughout the Mackenzie basin by a network of trading posts and missions. In the early 1900s, up to two tonnes of salt were gathered annually.

The Salt Plains form a truly unusual natural environment that invites the adventurous to visit during any of the four seasons. Unique in Canada, the plains are preserved as part of Wood Buffalo National Park, itself a World Heritage Site.

Upper: *Red samphire and Nuttall's salt-meadow grass border Brine Creek.*
Lower: *After days of rain, much of the Salt Plains rest under water. Salt deposits are dissolved and transported into the waterways.*

An aerial view of the Salt Plains reveals the shape of islands of salt-stressed spruce casting their evening shadows on the mud flats, where the soil is too saline and bare for plant life to grow.

Upper: *Salt-tolerant plants like red samphire border the mud flats, followed by salt-resistant plants like Nuttall's salt-meadow grass.*
Lower: *A view of the Salt Plains from the top of the escarpment.*

The tracks of birds and mammals, like these bear tracks, record who has travelled the mud flats since the last heavy rain.

ome of the oldest rock in the world is found in the taiga shield, exposed as giant precambrian outcrops worn smooth by erosion, or as monolithic bluffs where peregrine falcons and eagles nest. Innumerable lakes nestle in glacially-carved depressions, connected by a maze of rushing rivers and streams. Long sinuous eskers break up the landscape. The uplands, with dry sparse soils, are interspersed by pockets of wetlands and open forests, as well as shrub-lands and meadows more common in the tundra. Caribou lichen and moss cling to rock surfaces bearing a thin dusting of soil.

More than fifty species of mammals live in the taiga shield - the transition zone between forest and tundra - including moose, wolf, fox, beaver, lynx, black bear and the migratory barrenground caribou. Hundreds of thousands of birds come to nest or feed on their way to tundra breeding grounds. Unfortunately, this vast tract of wilderness is also rich in diamonds and other minerals and is attracting considerable exploration and development.

Scoured by glaciers that retreated about 10,000 years ago, the smooth surface of a rock outcrop in the Precambrian shield reflects the midnight sun.

Monolithic rock bluffs plummet into the Taltson River in shield country. Evidence of higher water levels in the past can be clearly seen at the base of the rock wall.

Upper: *A canoeing paradise in the subarctic wilderness of the Taiga Shield.*
Lower: *A natural garden of sunburst lichen, surrounded mainly by rock tripe and caribou lichen, clings to a rock of the Canadian Shield.*

Lower: *Cracks, crevasses and depressions are among the many pockets in shield country that capture and retain fine grains from erosion, decomposing plant matter and moisture, creating a fertile environment for new growth.*

30

Upper: *A young river otter demonstrates characteristic curiosity.*
Lower: *The leading edge of an active dune encroaches on the boreal forest at the Athabasca Sand Dunes, in the far northwest of Saskatchewan.*

In contrast to the green boreal forest, shades of butterscotch show the varying depths of water over the sand bottom of the William River as it cuts through the Athabasca Sand Dunes.

The Athabasca Sand Dunes are like no other place I have ever experienced. No sign of humans and their industrialized world. Just nature, free to run its course. They are a place of worship and peace - worship of life in nature and peace within.

As we hike barefoot from the sandy shore of Lake Athabasca, great expanses of uniformly-spaced rocks appear before us, floating on sand. Large sand bowls and flat dunes harbour fields of stones, carefully arranged and worn smooth by wind and sand. Small areas are dotted by tiny pebbles, while larger ones resemble widely spaced cobblestones, a phenomenon known as Gobi pavement.

Our route is dotted with pockets of pulpy grasses, succulents and mint green fern-like plants covered in silver fuzz. Weird willows with their gnarly roots exposed by the wind look like wine-coloured snakes slithering to the sky.

On the leeward edge of a dune the sand spills into the boreal forest. Where the two worlds meet, the trees are dead or dying, buried at the base by the encroaching sand. Most have had their weakened trunks snapped in half by wind sweeping off the dunes.

Approaching the William River, we walk through a skeletal forest of weathered, grey tree trunks protruding from the sand, mercilessly sculpted by wind and sand. They are all that remains of a once-thriving boreal forest.

The river itself stands in sharp contrast to the deep green of the surrounding forest, an intricate flowing pattern of a million tones of rich butterscotch. It makes the mouth water.

The Athabasca Sand Dunes cover some 1300 square kilometres and appear as a white splotch on satellite photographs. The dunes have been designated a provincial park.

Descending from the summit of a large dune is like walking a serpent's back as it snakes away into the distance.

Like nature's compass, wind circles are inscribed in the sand by long, bent blades of grass blowing in the wind.

Smoke from distant fires fills the sky for hundreds of miles, casting unusual light on the windswept peaks of the Athabasca Sand Dunes. The leeward side of the dune forms a perfect angle of repose, the maximum steepness the grain size of the sand can support. Even the slightest disturbance, human or animal, would upset the fine balance of this perfectly sloping wall of sand.

Upper: *Evenly spaced stones of "Gobi Pavement" and a clump of moss campion past its prime.*
Lower: *Unique and hardy plants have adapted to survive in this sea of sand.*

Skeletal remnants of a diminishing pine forest in the Athabasca Sand Dunes. Desiccated and ravaged by wind-blown sand, they are a testimonial to the active nature of the dune field.

An icy bay on the Slave River near Fort Smith. Despite consecutive days of temperatures below -30°C, the dynamic energy of the river and the turbulence of the rapids keeps the water in this bay open throughout winter. Mist rises from the surface of the open water into the cold winter air, creating clouds of fog that drift above the forested river banks.

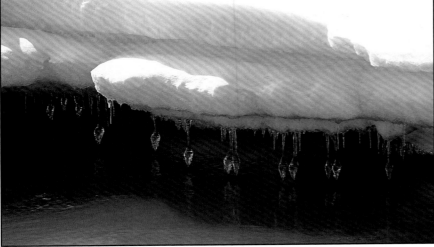

Upper: *Most of the barrenground caribou herds winter inside the treeline.*
Lower: *Nature's ornaments formed by the ebb and flow of the river.*

The top layer of the snow pack is sculpted by wind. The strengths of various layers are affected by pressures and temperatures in the snow pack and the air temperature during initial precipitation.

The beauty of an ice-laden trapper's cabin is also an indication of poor insulation. Although snow has excellent insulating properties, heat from inside transforms the snow to ice, which is a very poor insulator. This is why snow shelters are for temporary use and need to be rebuilt regularly.

The low angle of the winter sun creates a landscape of enchanting reflections, deep shadows and refracted beams as it bounces off crystals of ice and snow. Reflected sunlight bathes the surroundings in bright light, while beams shoot upward from the ice, and ice-coated branches are back-lit by the sun.

As the sun nears the horizon, an array of warm hues fills the sky. A profusion of pink and purple or orange and yellow tones silhouette scrubby spruce, thick boreal forest, smooth undulating shield rock, or wide frozen lakes and rivers.

With a wide range of colours, skylines, cloud formations and light phenomena, no two sunsets are alike in the Forgotten North.

Upper: *In the late afternoon sunset of early winter, the open water of Kakisa Lake dusts the bare deciduous branches with hoar frost.*
Lower: *Winter nights come alive with the aurora borealis dancing overhead.*

A trapper's cabin is blessed by one of the most spectacular natural phenomena on earth. Watching an auroral display is like watching a great spirit capriciously painting the dark sky with electric green light. Huge swaths and fine filaments can be intense at the onset, then fade quickly or sometimes linger.

In Dogrib legend, Ithenhiela fled on a caribou that used magic to throw obstacles in the path of a relentless pursuer. The caribou created hills from a lump of earth, muskeg from a patch of moss, forest from a branch and the Rocky Mountains from a stone. At the end of their journey, Ithenhiela pulled a forbidden arrow from a tree and was carried to the sky, where he has lived ever since. The aurora that appears in the northern sky is Ithenhiela's fingers moving about.

Scientists believe the northern lights are created by electrically charged particles carried by solar winds. When the charged particles pass by the earth, some enter the earth's magnetic field and are guided toward the polar regions. There the particles interact with gases present in the atmosphere and release energy that is seen as the glow of the northern lights.

Whatever one believes, the northern lights are a compensating splendour in the long, cold winters of the Forgotten North. Lights fill the dark night like capricious flames of raging fire sprawling across the sky, moving with the speed of light and the flow of a whimsical ballerina. Countless particles move as if brilliantly choreographed, dancing in an ever-changing symphony of light and color. Cold and darkness fade away as the lights lift the soul and rekindle the spirit.

The play of light in the subarctic sky also occurs during the day. Sun dogs, sun pillars and halos occur when sunlight passes through ice fog at altitudes of 5,000 to 15,000 metres, with billions of crystals acting like tiny prisms, refracting and reflecting sunlight. Sun pillars usually occur in extremely cold air at sunrise and sunset when a beam of sunlight reflects off the bottom of plate shaped crystals with angular edges. Sun dogs are created when sunlight enters the sides of plate crystals and is refracted twice inside.

Upper: *Sundogs appear in the late afternoon of a cold winter day.*
Lower: *A sun pillar emerges from the horizon, piercing the cloud cover.*

The scarlet aurora borealis is a rare phenomenon that last occurred on the night of March 23, 1991. Experts say the unusual color is caused by powerful solar winds hitting the earth's magnetic field and causing a "great magnetic storm." The winds, moving in excess of 1000 kilometres per second, are in turn caused by an unusually massive solar flare.

Capturing the northern lights on film takes a combination of luck and experience. The essentials are a manual camera with a tripod, a fast film and a night sky with a vivid aurora. Then the photographer has to guess how bright the aurora are and how long to hold the shutter open. Often the photographs have white flecks in them. These are bright stars that move during long film exposures.

The unusual color and awesome expanse of the rare red aurora is momentous enough for some to believe it was caused by a huge explosion or fire, or that the world was coming to an end.

Depending on temperature, weather and timing, the short autumn can be colourful, vibrant and warm one year, and dreary, wet and bone-chilling the next.

The setting sun illuminates the gnarled outline of ice-coated branches, where willow forests sprawl among the moister areas of the boreal forest. These areas are prime habitat for moose, which feed on the young buds and tender shoots.

The twisted silhouette of a white birch contrasts with the rigid landscape of the Canadian Shield. The flexible, waterproof bark was traditionally used for making canoes, baskets and other containers.

Contrary to southern perceptions, summer in the Forgotten North is usually very dry and warm, with temperatures often above 30°C. Days can last 19 to 24 hours at their peak, depending on latitude, giving subarctic vegetation an essential period of accelerated growth. Silently paddling a canoe through these seemingly never-ending hours of dusk-turning-to-dawn is a spiritual experience.

The people of this land are busiest during the long days of summer, making maximal use of the extended daylight. People travel out on the land, gather and prepare foodstuffs for the inevitable winter, and simply reconnect with the land. Sleep becomes a low priority, purely a consequence of physical need.

Autumn can be intensely beautiful and dramatically short, with orange, red, and yellow running rampant through the mixed forests, busy understory and open ground. Each year is different, depending on when the first frost comes, how severe it is and how long it stays. Small changes in weather patterns can have an enormous impact on this brief, fickle, subarctic season.

Winter is long and cold, but it is a welcome season for many people, a time to rest a weary body after the busy summer days, to hibernate and to reconnect with extended family and friends. It is also a time of magical beauty and extraordinary light, as the aurora dances for hours in the night sky.

Spring is eagerly anticipated and always welcome, lifting the spirits of the people and beckoning them out into the warmer but still sub-zero temperatures. By March, each day can be 8 minutes longer than the last and soon the snow is melting and giving way to an explosion of growth. Tight buds burst into vibrant green leaves in only a few days, as the land awakens to a new year.

The serenity of this scene is thwarted in reality by the constant buzz of hungry insects bouncing off the bug netting. Sunset is a prime time for these tiny beasts because the heat of the midday has subsided and the wind has vanished.

Upper: *Autumn signals impending repose for much of nature.*
Lower: *A duckling at dusk without the protection and guidance if its mother is easy quarry for predators.*

Typical of rivers in the Forgotten North, break-up on the Hay River sends huge slabs of ice onto the banks, where they slowly melt in the warming sun to form candled ice.

Upper: *In spring, the massive expanse of ice on Great Slave Lake creates heavy fog over the warmer landscape at its shores.*
Lower: *Candled ice tinkles and chimes as it falls from slabs of river ice.*

The sun is low in the sky during the daylight hours of winter, casting long, dark shadows across the untouched snow. The striped patterns and the subtle tones of grey have a calming effect in the deep quiet of winter.

Along time ago, an old woman asked her people for a meal of beaver blood but times were hard and they could not provide it. In despair, she sat down by a falls and was swept away in the current, never to be seen again. The spirit of the woman returned as a rainbow that watches over the falls to this day.

Places of danger are often associated with stories such as this, reminding people to ask for help and guidance from their powerful Creator. At Alexandra Falls the spirits of an old man and woman care for the waters. People make offerings of tobacco, matches, tea or bullets at the falls and pray for help in leading a good life. If a rainbow appears, the spirits are looking kindly on you. If a rainbow does not appear, the spirits are unhappy and something bad might happen.

Upper: *An old woman's spirit appears as a rainbow in the mist of the falls.*
Lower: *In the depths of the caverns, a goddess figure is created as the sun casts dark shadows on the towering limestone walls of the Hay River Gorge.*

A thin ledge of disintegrated rock and organic remains has enough nutrients to support a small ecosystem between the river's edge and the canyon walls.

As I walk along the Twin Falls Trail, I can hear the intense roar of Alexandra Falls dropping 36 metres over a precipitous limestone cliff into the Hay River Gorge. Hearing the falls before seeing them, enhances one's comprehension of the sheer volume of the water and the power that can be created by nature.

From Louise Falls to Alexandra Falls, the three kilometre Twin Falls trail winds its way through distinct pockets of jack pine, spruce, and mixed forest of white spruce and trembling aspen.

A 36-metre drop over the limestone ledge at Alexandra Falls marks the beginning of the spectacular Hay River gorge. This 25-kilometre stretch of water flows between golden walls up to 50 metres high and through ancient geological formations as beautiful as they are unique. At the 2-kilometre mark, the calm river is interrupted by a further 16-metre drop at Louise Falls.

Limestone cliffs along the route are gradually crumbling under the onslaught of time and erosion. Tall columns of limestone have calved from the sides, many topped with a patch of forest that has slowly adjusted to the changing angle of the earthen surface on the fragile pillar. High up on the gorge walls, tree trunks are literally splitting in half as new slabs of limestone slowly break away from the cliffs. Deep caverns and crevasses cast bright light and dark shadows on the cliff walls. Scree slopes lie heaped against the base of the walls.

The Hay River basin contains no natural storage, so runoff patterns show great seasonal variation. In spring, huge volumes of water crash over the edge of the limestone shelves. At times, a thick mist rises into the air, welling up from the base of the falls and filling the gorge before dissipating over the treetops. By the end of a very dry summer, the falls have dwindled into dozens of tiny rivulets, highlighting the finer notches in the limestone ledges.

The first long icicles form on the sides of Alexandra Falls in early winter and gradually, as temperatures drop, the falls freeze over, until the remaining flow thunders off the ledge and into a hole in a mound of ice. Mist from this last stream of open water floats into the air and gathers at the top of the falls, forming a peak like a shark's snout rising from the water, its jagged jaws of icicles outlining its open steaming throat.

Upper: *Curiosity overcomes the fear of a river otter surprised by the sight of a visitor it cannot hear over the roar of the rapids.*
Lower: *Louise Falls transforms into cascading rivulets after a long dry summer.*

Pure stands of trembling aspen can be found in the rich, fertile soils of moist depressions. Considered a weather indicator by some, leaves shimmering in the absence of any perceptible wind signal a storm is on its way.

Upper: *A ruffed grouse chick has not yet mastered the skill of flight.*
Lower: *Ancient coralite fossils can be found in the rubble slopes of Escarpment Creek.*

The second of two falls on Escarpment Creek cascades over the predominantly limestone and shale cliffs that record 450 million years of geological history. Northern sweet vetch, or wild sweet pea, adorns a talus slope that tumbles into the amphitheater-shaped basin of the falls .

Upper: *Trappers' cabins dot the wilderness within the treeline.*
Lower: *Lichen clings to a small protrusion in the bark of a birch tree.*

Early in the winter, water still flows at Escarpment Creek, creating a frozen world of fantastical ice formations.

The fishbowl-shaped canyon of the second falls appears before us as a fabulous world of white, a fantasia of free flowing water spilling over frozen mounds of stepped cascades. Spray splatters from the rushing water and mist floats into the crisp, cold air. We feel the tingling chill on our faces as we venture into the depths of this winter wonderland, first to the back of the fishbowl beneath the overhanging falls, then down the canyon, following the creek as it flows beneath the ice.

Variations in cold northern temperatures cause moisture to form different crystalline structures, creating a multitude of uniquely artistic ice formations in the canyon of Escarpment Creek. Mist deposited on the back wall beneath the overhanging falls forms long, thick stalactite features that look like matted sheep's tails. Further downstream, meringue-like pillars of frozen froth emerge from openings where turbulent water has kept the ice at bay. They are formed as froth rises in the cold air, freezes and is in turn pushed up by more froth, building pillars up to a metre high on the creek's icy surface.

Throughout the winter, various stages of freeze-up occur at the waterfalls on Escarpment Creek, as well as most of the other falls along the geological formation known as the Alexandra Escarpment. The process usually starts in November and by spring most of the falls have become frozen cascades of solid ice.

Upper: *A frozen mound of stepped cascades builds under the falling water.*
Lower: *Spray and mist from the falling water freezes onto the overhanging limestone cliff, like a wall of long, matted sheep's tails.*

At Lady Evelyn Falls on the Kakisa River, grandiose ice falls appear on the side wall in winter, where only insignificant trickles of water can be found in spring and summer.

Upper: *The autumn colours of balsam poplar, willow and trembling aspen leaves litter the ground for a short time before the first snow falls.*
Lower: *High-bush cranberry, or mooseberry, makes delectable jams and jellies.*

An observer provides a true sense of scale against the grandeur of Wallace Creek's last drop over the escarpment.

The day after the fire, sweeping lines emphasizing the lay of the land can be seen in the pattern of the burn.

Upper: *The degree of disturbance from the last burn is revealed in the vegetation patterns of the regenerating forest.*
Lower: *A few lonely jackpine stand among the regrowth from deciduous roots.*

The Dene traditionally had a thorough understanding of natural factors affecting fires. In the past, they set controlled fires in specific locations to encourage the kinds of animals and edible plants they liked to harvest.

Fire is essential to the natural succession of boreal forest, with most areas burning about once every 100 years, changing the nature of the forest floor and making way for regeneration. Natural fires leave patchy disturbance patterns and a variety of organic debris. Some fires are very hot, opening the cones of jackpine and releasing the seeds. Other fires burn at lower temperatures, allowing deciduous trees to grow back from roots left in the ground.

Despite claims to the contrary, current logging practices do not approximate the complex processes of natural forest fires.

Forest fires are left to run their natural course unless human assets are threatened. The CL-215 is the world's only aircraft designed as a water-scooping bomber and can scoop 5000 litres in 10 seconds, dropping it over a fire in only one second.

Intensely coloured sunsets are created when heavy smoke from forest fires fills the air. Often smoke is so dense that even the midday sun is filtered and transformed into an orange ball.

The spectacular waterfalls cascading off the series of escarpments along the south side of the upper Mackenzie River, between the Hay River and the Trout River, are the result of ancient geological activity on a continental scale. In pre-glacial times, about 2 million years ago, major drainages in this region flowed east toward Hudson Bay, completely opposite to the flow of the modern upper Mackenzie River. These pre-glacial rivers cut through hundreds of metres of older sedimentary rock and widened the ancient valleys. The nature of sedimentary rock strata varies greatly. Weaker layers offer little resistance to erosion, resulting in rapid widening of the valley. More resistant layers are less easily eroded, producing escarpments within the broad valley system.

The situation gradually changed as the Laurentide Ice Sheet advanced westward from plateaus near Hudson Bay, blocking the east-flowing rivers and forcing them to find alternate routes. The ice ultimately reached the Mackenzie Mountains and re-directed all drainage north to the Beaufort Sea. The modern Mackenzie River was established as the ice sheet retreated, making the Mackenzie one of the world's largest glacially-implaced drainage systems.

Today, tributaries of the Mackenzie River, including the Hay River, Trout River, Wallace Creek, McNallie Creek and Escarpment Creek, all run north, generally perpendicular to the old drainage valley and its escarpments, inevitably forming numerous waterfalls.

Layers that make up the escarpments, deposited by ancient seas some 460 million years ago, vary in thickness and hardness. Relentless water erosion has worn weaker layers and left more resistant ones, giving each waterfall a unique configuration.

Upper: *Lofty trembling aspen flourish in the rich soils of the boreal forest.*
Lower: *In spring, last year's young beaver are forced out of the family unit to find their own territory.*

Upper: *Several geological layers of fossils can be found around Samba Deh Falls. Most fossils date back to the Palaeozoic era.*
Lower: *The raging shoot of Samba Deh Falls on the Trout River.*

Still groggy from winter hibernation, this bear showed its youthfulness in curious, unalarmed behaviour. In a seemingly playful gesture, he nibbled at the dry dead weed in front of him.

Contrary to popular belief, porcupine do not throw their quills. In the face of a perceived threat, they swiftly twist their bodies and flick their tails, jabbing their barbed quills in defense.

Upper: *The bare Trout River canyon is stripped of soil deposits at high water.* Lower: *A variety of rock compositions and structures create distinctly different configurations of rock and water along the Trout River canyon.*

Low water at the upper falls of the Trout River spills out of eroded basins and hollows and over the ledge. The aggregate of the shelf fractures easily into small round fragments, creating smoother, more rounded features and contours.

Downstream from Samba Deh Falls, the Trout River canyon can be accessed through a deep narrow crevasse that culminates in this hidden Shangri-La deep within the canyon walls.

A bull caribou poses majestically, with his stark, white "bell" blowing in the north wind. Caribou migrate from the barrenlands back into the treeline in autumn.

Well-worn paths in the blanket of vegetation, sun bleached antlers, lichen tufts chewed down to the ground, and this back bone are all signs of caribou migration.

Upper: *A caribou trail cuts through a patch of forest on the crest of an esker.*
Lower: *The growth of the tundra vegetation shows that this antler must have been resting here for years.*

It is the final day of our three week journey down the Thelon River and we have seen only a single one of the thousands, or even hundreds of thousands, of caribou that usually migrate through this area. Engrossed in thought, I wander around the archeological site surrounding our camp, stepping over stones that once circled the caribou hide tents of inland Inuit. Sun-bleached bone fragments and small rock chips lie scattered about, left behind in the tool-making process. I think about the harsh life these people must have lead.

A low, repetitive noise distracts me from my thoughts. Probably a goose, I think... or maybe a few geese or... what is that noise? I look up and across the river to the opposite bank. There are too many caribou to count. Larger ones, smaller ones, frisky little calves, coated in light beige, white or rusty brown. Grunts, snorts and clicks fill my ears from a thousand animals. They are the most intense sounds I have heard during our trip. It is like nothing I could have imagined.

The Chipewyan say that "no one knows the way of the wind and the caribou." Meat, blood and stomach contents from these animals traditionally provided a balanced diet for native people. Antler, bone and sinew were used to make tools, weapons and ornaments. Skins were used for tents, bedding and clothing. Even the nomadic movement of the people was guided by the seasonal migration of the caribou. The migratory whims of the caribou no longer mean life or death but caribou retain significant economic value and spiritual importance to the people of the Forgotten North.

When humans approach, the gregarious caribou run a short distance, then stop and turn for another look, their heads perky and their soft white muzzles pointing. Then they trot jauntily away, dismissing the threat. One winter I dressed in a white sheet and tried to sneak up on a small herd but they were not fooled. Four individuals pranced back and forth in front of me, as if to see if I would chase them, then wandered off unconcerned.

The synchronized gait of caribou gracefully prancing across Thekulthili Lake near the Taltson River in shield country sends a distinct clicking sound into the crisp cold air. This characteristic sound is caused by tendons slipping over the sesamoid bone in their feet as they walk.

A rough-legged hawk circles and cries 'keeer' over its cliff-side nest as a canoe passes under wing.

Upper: *A huge population of geese molt over several weeks in the Thelon Oasis.* Lower: *Stratified with weaker layers, rocks are eroded into uniform patterns by trapped moisture and freeze-thaw action.*

An esker left behind by the Laurentide Ice Sheet some 9, 000 years ago stands in stark contrast to a pocket of the boreal forest. This pocket, set in a sea of barren tundra, makes the Thelon Wildlife Sanctuary unique.

A cliff top view of the crystal-clear water of a Thelon River tributary.

lders refer to it as "the place where god began when the world was created." Thousands of muskoxen roam free, wolves live their lives without learning to fear humans and hundreds of thousands of caribou migrate to secluded calving grounds in the vast wilderness. Countless geese and swans molt and nest, while peregrine falcons, rough-legged hawks and gyrfalcons raise their young on sheer cliffs that fall away to the clear blue waters of the Thelon River. Barrenland grizzlies roam supreme, while arctic ground squirrels, known as sic-sics, cavort close to their dens.

In the Thelon Wildlife Sanctuary, I become a member of the wildlife population, just another creature living in the wilderness. One day I follow a wolf who is fully aware of my presence. She pauses to listen at a willow shrub, then pounces and sends a ptarmigan bursting forth in a flurry of excitement. Next she saunters along a gully, stops about 10 metres away, observes me for a minute or two, then casually goes about her business. There is no fear and no aggression, just plain curiosity.

I know from the scent that muskoxen are near. They will let me approach in plain view but if I hide behind shrubs and sneak up on them, they flee in a cloud of dust and thundering hooves.

One day my mother and I sight a moose fleeing into thick willows, and she decides to try and flush him out. A rustling sound emanates from the willows. "What are you doing in here?" she asks, somewhat surprised. "I'm not in there," I reply, trying to get a better look. I climb onto a mound of sand to find a set of soft velvety horns peeking out over the ratty willow tops. The moose studies me for a while, then flees as my mother emerges from the willows with a big goose in her arms, its head buried in her elbow as if trying to hide.

Despite the abundance of wildlife, nature has its own ideas, as John Hornby and his party discovered in 1927. They had planned to winter on the Thelon but starved to death because they failed to consider migratory patterns of the caribou.

A pink splash of alpine azalea blossoms hugs a lichen-covered boulder. The minute leathery leaves of this matted dwarf shrub are coated by a waxy substance that reduces water loss in the dry tundra climate. The first flower to bloom on the barrenlands in spring, it can be found exposed to the sun beside patches of melting snow.

The start of a wilderness expedition. Float planes drop off adventurers and their supplies far out in the tundra, at the edge of the Thelon Wildlife Sanctuary.

Upper: *Muskoxen like to feed on new growth of willow, leaving qiviut, their soft under hair, snagged on branches and blowing in the tundra breeze.*
Lower: *A rough-legged hawk's nest on a cliff over the Hanbury River.*

Hand crafted by an ancestor of the present-day Dene, this arrowhead or spear tip from the late Taltheilei period could be a thousand years old. The side notching feature of this artifact dates back to as early as 800 A.D.

Upper: *Moss campion grows in tight mats of tiny leaves and flowers, deeply anchored by its tap-root and pressed over rock and sand.*
Lower: *A gyrfalcon chick, a member of the largest falcon species in the world.*

Upper: *The agile, graceful arctic tern is the longest migrator in the world.*
Lower: *Mountain avens rotate to face the sun 24 hours a day, making the most of the short northern summers.*

The river at Beverly Lake has left the farthest reaches of the treeline and flows out into the barrenlands. This area was a meeting place of the Inuit and Chipewyan, as they followed the barrenground caribou to the calving grounds just north of the Lake. Ironically it wasn't until the last day of our 22-day journey, while among the archeological remnants of one of these ancient hunting camps, that we saw our first and only caribou herd.

Arock cairn on a knoll above Parry Falls is surrounded by scrubby spruce adorned with colourful fragments of cloth, left as offerings by those who have come to experience the healing power of the waters. The spiritual ambiance is enhanced by a campfire puffing smoke into the air.

Every year in early August, Dene from all over the region make a pilgrimage to this sacred site, a place of awesome natural power, rich with cultural and spiritual significance. Here they make offerings and ask the spirit of the old woman who watches over the falls to help them lead a good and healthy life.

Those who need healing stay at the falls for a night or two, while the others camp at the lake nearby, praying that those remaining at the falls receive what they ask. Dene youth come to learn the traditional ways, to gain knowledge of the land and to hear the stories of their people, their elders and their ancestors.

This elder travelled hundreds of kilometres by plane, boat and trail to reach Parry Falls, where she will drink from the healing waters and participate in a healing ceremony.

The flow of the Lockhart River is bent in two places by a spectacular configuration of sheer cliffs, giving rise to the 42-metre drop at Parry Falls. The congregation on the rock knoll at the top of the falls provides a striking sense of scale.

A tight clump of saxifrage, which in Latin means "rock breaker," spills over the incline like a natural rockery garden, rooting itself in crevices bulging with soil and organic remains. The succulent basal leaves, in the form of rosettes, turn orange and red after the shock of the first frost.

Redcliff Island, The Gap, Fortress Island and McDonald Cliff are part of an extensive series of breath-taking formations along the East Arm of Great Slave Lake. In sharp contrast to the adjacent rugged glaciated granite and gneiss country, the folded sedimentaries and volcanics of the East Arm produce a landscape of gentle slopes that end in dramatic drops into the water, like the 225-metre cliff on Etthen Island. The central part of the East Arm includes Christie Bay, where extraordinarily clear water descends over 600 metres, making it the deepest fresh water in North America.

Located at the edge of the barrenlands, the unique ecological transition zone surrounding the East Arm includes thick boreal forest and expanses of rock, which give way to tundra within tens of kilometres of the lake. This area is being considered for a national park.

Upper: *Where there is little contact with humans, wolves express their curious nature without aggression or fear.*
Lower: *Alpine bearberry splashes the tundra and forest floor with red.*

In the East Arm, many of the shorelines are sheer rock cliffs that plummet into the depths of Great Slave Lake. At 614 metres, it is the deepest lake in Canada.

The cliffs of the Douglas Peninsula provide calm waters in a small inlet of Wildbread Bay, on the East Arm of Great Slave Lake.

This is the original southern boundary of the Thelon Game Sanctuary, created in 1927 for the protection of muskoxen and barrenground caribou. The boundary was moved farther north in 1956 due to mining interests in the area . Today, the fate of the Thelon Wildlife Sanctuary rests in the hands of the Dene and Inuit who both have a stake in its management.

A flight over the "treeline" reveals a zone of gradual ecological transition rather than a precise demarcation. Initially, spaces begin to appear among the trees, exposing fields of mint green lichen interspersed by patches of exposed sand left behind by glacial streams about 9,000 years ago.

Eskers rise above the vast flatland, providing low relief as they wind their way like serpents through the landscape, forming beautiful sandy beaches on the shores of numerous lakes.

Trees become fewer in number and shorter in stature until only a few small, gnarled trees hang on in isolated clumps. Then they too defer to the endless barrenland tundra, with its riddled maze of lakes, rivers, polygons, boulder fields, rock outcrops and occasional sprawling eskers.

In biological terms, the "treeline" is the edge of the continuous forest that delineates the subartic from the tundra community.

Crossing the treeline by air verifies a dwindling forest. The exposed sand of the esker can be seen in patches on the sprawling mat of lichen.

The previous year's fronds of the fragrant shield fern dry out and curl up at the base of the plant, forming a protective layer against erosion and moisture loss.

Upper: *The Franklin Mountains loom majestically over the breadth of the Mackenzie valley along the road to Wrigley.*
Lower: *An immature bald eagle takes flight, evading our canoe.*

Death by natural causes, including predation, is both a reality and a necessity because it preserves the balance of the remote wilderness ecosystem. This wolf died of unknown causes.

The immensity of the Mackenzie River and its tributaries is almost unfathomable. Together they drain a basin covering 1.8 million square kilometres and stretching 4,241 kilometres from its uppermost reaches to the Beaufort Sea. It ranks seventh in the world in terms of flow, behind only the Mississippi and the Amazon in the western hemisphere.

Southwest of the basin lie the Mackenzie Mountains, rich with natural treasures: the Ram Plateau, with its majestic karst valleys that drop vertically from broad plateaus; the Cirque of the Unclimbables, batholithic protrusions that pierce the heavens; and the Nahanni, river of myth and magic. Serious adventurers can follow the Canol Trail through deep canyons, rugged mountains, and alpine tundra from the Northwest Territories to the Yukon, via Macmillan Pass.

Upper: *At their confluence, the silt-laden waters of the Liard River contrast with the black waters of the Pettitot, at the edge of the settlement of Fort Liard.*
Lower: *The Liard Range of the Mackenzie Mountains provides a grand backdrop for this Liard valley autumn vista.*

Sheer rock bluffs interrupt the flow of the Nahanni River, bending it 90 degrees and giving rise to the challenging whitewater of the Figure 8 Rapids, also known as Hell's Gate. This calm eddy is created in its wake, allowing paddlers to regroup and regain their composure.

Although not ideal weather for canoeing, a fresh snow fall in late August highlights the features of the terrain.

The Nahanni River appears as a faint silver ribbon through the mist below. Spectacular views are bestowed on hikers who scale the lofty heights of mountain summits along the river valley.

The Nahanni River explodes, sending spray and mist into the air as it crashes into Mason Rock, which divides the cataclysmic waters of Virginia Falls. The entire drop of the falls, a total of 117 metres from Sluice Box Rapids into Five Mile Canyon, is twice the height of Niagara Falls.

We awake on a brisk morning late in August to find the landscape under a heavy, wet blanket of white, the first snowfall of the year on the shores of the Nahanni River. Even the extra gear we packed just in case of snow does little to protect us from the bitterly cold wind blowing up the river corridor. Our wet hands become numb from exposure as we paddle, making the late summer trip almost unbearable.

Despite the inhospitable cold, the fresh snow adds a nuance of alluring beauty to the already dramatic scenery, accentuating the folds, stratifications and other features of the massive mountains along the river valley, and giving depth to the layers of forest rising into the distance. Changing temperatures form brooding mists that rise from the valley floor. Then the sun emerges from behind dark clouds and we rejoice as golden sunlight illuminates the sheer walls of the canyon.

There is magic in the Nahanni and all it embraces. Dusty beige carbonate tuffa mounds emerge from the dark boreal forest, the majestic Ragged Range with the Cirque of the Unclimbables juts into the sky and steamy hot springs beckon the weary traveller. Virginia Falls is one of North America's wonders, its raging water split in half by a giant pillar, then crashing into the canyon below.

On one 50-kilometre stretch, the swift, meandering river is guided along by a series of canyons with walls up to 1.5 kilometres high. This unique section of river was formed by the uplift of mountains, concurrent with entrenchment of an already existing flat, meandering waterway. Narrow tributary canyons join the main river via smooth, undulating spillways that leave perfect bathing pools. Caves dot the omnipresent rock walls, holding hidden secrets deep within.

No wonder the myth, magic and mystery of this place has been revered by generations of native people, explorers and prospectors. Today the Nahanni offers a journey of a lifetime, a journey into rugged wilderness and a journey within oneself, reconnecting the spirit to the earth, grounding the heart, body, mind and soul.

In the shadow of the mountain, morning mist rises from the valley floor through a cluster of dying spruce rooted at the edge of a coarsely segregated alluvial fan.

Upper Left: *A ruffed grouse searches for a new territory in the early snow.*
Upper Right: *The Figure 8 Rapids deceptively appear as mere ripples in the river when viewed from the portage trail traversing the heights of the cliff above.*
Lower: *Late August, and the first snow has come early in the Mackenzie Mountains. At higher elevations, features will remain under a blanket of white until spring.*

The view across the Liard River from Blackstone Park is the perfect setting to contemplate the end of a fourteen-day wilderness journey through the wilds of the Nahanni River. Nahanni Butte emerges from the horizon, marking the confluence of the Nahanni and Liard Rivers.

The Dempster Highway winds its way up and down through the Richardson Mountains. This region is characterized by two ecoregions: smooth alpine slopes of tundra at higher elevations, consisting of lichens, mountain avens, dwarf shrubs, sedges and arctic cotton; and valleys of subalpine open woodland vegetation such as stunted spruce, willow, dwarf birch, and Labrador tea with sedge, moss, and arctic cotton in moist depressions.

The Dempster Highway winds its way up and down numerous passes in the Richardson and Ogilvie Mountains, through mostly untouched wilderness between Inuvik at the northern limit of the treeline and Dawson City, deep within the boreal forest. Wide valleys, mountain bands, narrow passes and waterways line the route as it passes through six separate eco-regions of mountains, plateaus and plains.

Grizzlies and black bears can be seen dining on plentiful berries that hug the ground. Porcupine caribou migrate down from the North Slope and across the highway. Such a pristine, ecologically diverse and scenic highway is a treat to enjoy.

The highway was built as a result of an initiative by the Diefenbaker government, known as "Roads to Resources". The name itself is cause to fear for the integrity of this pristine wilderness.

South of Eagle Plains, the vegetation cover of the rounded hills creates a stark contrast to the bare rock features of a band of mountains across the wide valley.

Upper: *The Tombstone Range rises behind the North Klondike River valley.* Lower: *On the Dempster Highway, the late evening sun paints the clouds of a dissipating storm.*

The Forgotten North hosts a diversity of aboriginal cultures, including Gwich'in, Inuvialuit and Metis, as well as various Dene peoples, such as the Chipewyan, Slavey, Dogrib, Hare, Nahanni, and Loucheux. The richness of their traditional ways persists today, with the people continuing to identify themselves in relationship to the land and the life it supports. Plants and animals provide the food, clothing, tools, and shelter essential to a good life.

Going out on the land is vital to a sense of well-being for these aboriginal cultures, who over centuries have developed a deep connection to, and respect for, the land on which they depend. This includes accepting the responsibility of caring for the land and its living creatures.

Upper: *The day after the first snow, an early morning mist rolls over the mountains north of Eagle Plains on the Dempster Highway.*
Lower: *Alpine vegetation in autumn on the south side of Wright Pass.*

Inuvialuit elder Persis Grueben prepares dry fish. Many traditions of the aboriginal people of the Forgotten North are still practiced today. For people like Persis, the traditional northern lifestyle is part of recent history. As a little girl, she remembers a nomadic subsistence lifestyle and travelling to the supply post and whaling station of Herschel Island.

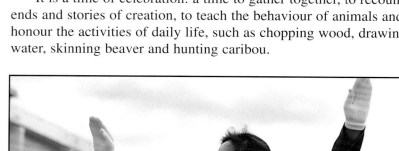

A steady clicking rhythm begins to fill the air surrounding the congregation, growing louder as more drummers follow the lead and tap their long, slender sticks on the rims of their broad caribou hide drums. Click, click, click, click. Dancers shuffle into the open area as the drummers pick up the volume, beating the entire width of the drum and adding a deep, resonating beat to the clicking. Dancers sweep their arms high and low, their wolverine fur fringes floating through the air. The dancers' souls are possessed by the spirit of their culture and this spirit spreads to the spectators. More and more dancers join in, creating a dizzying pattern of contrasting colour as they sway, dip and spin to the beat of many drums.

It is a time of celebration: a time to gather together, to recount legends and stories of creation, to teach the behaviour of animals and to honour the activities of daily life, such as chopping wood, drawing water, skinning beaver and hunting caribou.

Upper: *A dancer's glove rests on an Inuvialuit drum after the festivity.*
Lower: *Dressed in a traditional parka adorned with Delta Braid and strips of wolverine fur, an elder woman enjoys the spirit of the drum dance.*

The spirit of the Inuvialuit people thrives in the drum dance of the Mackenzie Delta Drummers and Dancers.

From the air or an elevated viewpoint it is relatively easy to trace a route through the maze of lakes and waterways that make up the Mackenzie delta. At water level, it is another world. The terrain is unrelentingly flat, the soil homogeneous and the vegetation uniform. Lofty boreal forest hides the Richardson Mountains from view, eliminating the only terrestrial reference point. Depth perception becomes confused, bearings are lost and even the direction of water flow can be uncertain. Years of experience are the only reliable guide to travel in the world's second largest arctic delta.

Unlike many of the world's great deltas, the 260,000 square kilometre Mackenzie delta is inaccessible and remote, creating a rich ecosystem in which wildlife flourishes. Migratory birds, fur-bearing animals and fish species are found in abundance.

Sand bars dotted with logs and driftwood mark the transition from the Mackenzie delta to the Beaufort Sea.

The second largest arctic river delta in the world, the Mackenzie delta's maze of lakes, channels, and main waterways is so complex, it can disorient even the most experienced wilderness travellers.

Moonrise over the Mackenzie Mountains creates a silver path down the Nahanni River, marking the end of a day's journey in the Forgotten North.

The end of a wilderness journey always seems to be marked by moments of extraordinary natural beauty: an electric pink sunset reflecting off the silver surface of a braided stream on a sand bar in the Thelon River; an encounter with a highly intelligent but very illusive wolverine traveling along the rocky river bank toward our canoe, its little black face peering out from behind a coat of long, flowing blonde hair; the beautiful overlap of moonrise and sunset, casting blues, purples and oranges across the sky, the colours and the breaking clouds reflecting off Four Mile Lake as our float plane descends to land; or the gathering of fifty loons around our boat, the sound of their calls echoing back and forth through the mist rising from the surface of the lake.

Often it is the last spectacular landscape of a journey that is etched in my mind, like the aerial view of the intricate butterscotch artistry of the William River as it meanders past the Athabasca Sand Dunes, or an autumn vista along the Dempster Highway, the multitude of bright colours against a smooth, sloping mountain backdrop.

Nostalgia sweeps over me as I retrace my steps and recount experiences at each leg of the journey - the stunning landscapes, the minute details of special rocks and plants, encounters with animals that seemed to communicate with me, the intimate friendships that developed between fellow travelers, and the feeling of reconnecting with the earth.

Although I find comfort in aspects of urban society, I always relive journeys of the past in my mind, in my photographs and in sharing experiences with others. Meanwhile, the wilderness beckons, urging me to make plans for the next journey.

In the darkness of the winter's afternoon, ptarmigan take flight like vanishing ghosts, evoking a sense of spirit within. They are like messengers of nature, sent to impress the spirit of the wilderness on the souls of all human beings, reconnecting us to the earth and to our part of the whole.

LESLIE LEONG

A four-day snowmobile trip had barely begun when Leslie abruptly stopped her machine, grabbed her camera and aimed at a snowy white ptarmigan hiding motionless beside the trail. The ptarmigan was camera-shy and moved deeper into the adjacent shrubland. As I watched in amusement, Leslie struggled after the cautious bird, wading through waist-deep snow in her bulky parka and soft leather mukluks, hoping for just the right angle and light conditions. The ptarmigan kept just out of range, its feathery feet walking easily on the soft snow. Forty-five minutes later the ptarmigan finally relented, having decided that this slow-moving, two-legged beast was really quite harmless. Leslie waded back to the trail, a triumphant smile on her face.

Outstanding photography takes not only a keen eye and a sense of artistic balance, but also determination, persistence and passion. Every photo in Leslie's collection is not only a work of art, but the result of countless hours of planning and packing, and weeks of remote isolation and natural hazards. Each photo is more than an isolated scene. It is a snapshot of the ongoing and enjoyable process that is the life of this talented photographer.

In the 20 years I have known Leslie, she has applied this same dedication to her travels. She took her first pictures on a trip along the newly opened Dempster Highway in 1979, where a sign still warned travelers that there was "No fuel, food or lodging for 542km." Subsequent trips took her throughout Taiwan, Turkey and Europe. Leslie's sense of adventure also lead her far into Canada's back country, including Baffin Island. Intrigued by the north, Leslie found a job in the Northwest Territories that combined her civil engineering background with her love for wilderness.

Leslie became a full-time photographer in 1994 and now devotes her time to recording the beauty and diversity of the natural world, hoping to instill in others her deep sense of passion and spiritual attachment to the environment.

Detmar Schwichtenberg

OUR FORGOTTEN NORTH

Photographer and Writer	Leslie Leong
Text Editor	Detmar Schwichtenberg
Design Consultant	Paradigm Graphic Design
Research, Design and Publisher	Leslie Leong Ent. Ltd.
Printer	Quality Color Press Ltd.

Upper Left: *Leslie photographing shield country in winter.*
Upper Right: *Looking for caribou on an esker at the edge of the treeline.*
Lower Left: *Leslie and son Tynan, with their dog, Wheeler.*
Lower Right: *Observing gyrfalcon fledglings at Hawk Rock on the Hanbury River.*